CHILDREN NEED
FAMILIES

Michael Pollard

THE WORLD'S CHILDREN

Children Need Education
Children Need Families
Children Need Food
Children Need A Future
Children Need Health Care
Children Need Homes
Children Need Recreation
Children Need Water

Book Editor: William Wharfe
Series Editor: Stephen White-Thomson
Designer: David Armitage
Consultants: Save the Children
Picture Editor: William Wharfe

All words that appear in **bold** in the text
are explained in the glossary on page 44

First published in 1988 by
Wayland (Publishers) Limited
61 Western Road, Hove
East Sussex BN3 1JD, England

© Copyright 1988 Wayland (Publishers) Limited

British Library Cataloguing in Publication Data
Pollard, Michael, 1931–
     Children need families (The World's Children)
     1. Families – For children
     I. Title   II. Series
     306.8'5   H327215

ISBN 1–85210–271–3

Phototypeset by Kalligraphics Ltd, Redhill, Surrey
Printed in Italy by G. Canale & C.S.p.A., Turin
Bound by Casterman S.A., Belgium

**Front cover: A family from Peru prepares to go to
work in the fields, except for the woman in the
centre of the picture, who is spinning wool.**

**Back cover: When posing for the camera, this little
girl from Nepal feels safe in her mother's arms.**

**Title page: This Egyptian grandmother enjoys the
company of her family: two sons, a daughter-in-
law, and two grandsons.**

**Contents page: When we are very young we rely
on our parents for almost everything. Sometimes
we are given a free ride – like the one this woman
from Thailand gives her daughter.**

CONTENTS

THE RIGHTS OF THE CHILD

Eglantine Jebb, the founder of The Save the Children Fund, drafted the Rights of the Child in 1923. It was revised in 1948 by the present Declaration of the Rights of the Child, commonly known as the Declaration of Geneva. These principles form the basis of our work and the Charter of The Save the Children Fund.

1 The Child must be protected beyond and above all considerations of race, nationality or creed.

2 The Child must be cared for with due respect for the family as an entity.

3 The Child must be given the means requisite for its normal development, materially, morally and spiritually.

4 The Child that is hungry must be fed, the child that is sick must be nursed, the child that is mentally or physically handicapped must be helped, the maladjusted child must be re-educated, the orphan and the waif must be sheltered and succoured.

5 The Child must be the first to receive relief in time of distress.

6 The Child must enjoy the full benefits provided by social welfare and social security schemes, must receive a training which will enable it, at the right time, to earn a livelihood, and must be protected against every form of exploitation.

7 The Child must be brought up in the consciousness that its talents must be devoted to the service of its fellow men.

BUCKINGHAM PALACE

All children, regardless of race, nationality or creed, have basic rights. These rights were outlined by Eglantine Jebb, the founder of Save the Children, in 1923 and they have now become an integral part of the United Nations charter. You can read them on the opposite page.

I welcome this thought-provoking series and applaud the way it confronts the issues facing today's children throughout the world. In the end we are all part of the same human race, and not so different from one another. Where differences do exist, they enrich us.

As Britain's largest international children's charity, Save the Children works where there is real need, both in the UK and in over 50 countries around the world. The idea behind all our projects is to encourage people to help themselves. But SCF also accepts its responsibility to talk about the issues of world-wide child poverty - particularly to the young - which makes this work so necessary. This series is designed to do just that.

I am sure that this colourful series will be an invaluable resource for any school whose aim is to make their pupils think beyond the confines of their playground and their community. We are one world after all. Let's try and be one.

Anne

WHY WE NEED FAMILIES

The idea of the family is important to all human beings. We grow up in families. When we become adults, most of us will start new families of our own. Living in family groups is the usual way of life for human beings. Having our families near us makes us feel safe. Members of our families are people we know and should be able to love and trust.

There are two differences between humans and other animals which help to make the human family more important.

First, it takes a long time for a child to learn the skills needed for **survival** in the adult world. A puppy or a kitten can learn all it needs from its mother in just a few weeks.

This little girl from Bali has a mother who cares for her and loves her. ▽

After that, it does not need its family any more. Children do not have enough **experience** to leave home until they are at least teenagers. They need the protection of the family while they are growing up.

The other big difference between humans and other animals is what happens when they become too old or ill to survive on their own. When this happens to an animal, it simply dies. But humans believe that they should look after old and sick people. The family provides a way of doing this.

Because the idea of the family has so much meaning for us, we often use the word 'family' to describe other kinds of **relationships** – such as between communities or even countries.

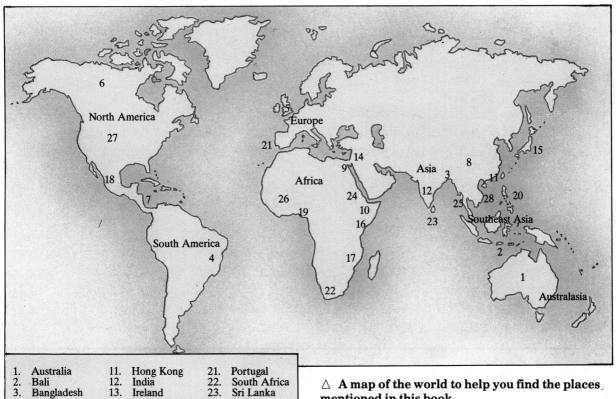

1. Australia	11. Hong Kong	21. Portugal
2. Bali	12. India	22. South Africa
3. Bangladesh	13. Ireland	23. Sri Lanka
4. Brazil	14. Israel	24. Sudan
5. Britain	15. Japan	25. Thailand
6. Canada	16. Kenya	26. Upper Volta
7. Carribean	17. Malawi	27. USA
8. China	18. Mexico	28. Vietnam
9. Egypt	19. Nigeria	
10. Ethiopia	20. Philippines	

△ **A map of the world to help you find the places mentioned in this book.**

People sometimes talk about 'the family of nations'. This seems to suggest that if people all over the world behaved as if they were in the same family, there would be less violence and war. Sadly, not all families are kind and loving, but we still believe that this is how they should be.

Cats look after their young for only a short time. Humans need to be looked after for much longer – after all, we have much more to learn! ▽

ALL IN THE FAMILY

Families are made up of people who are related to one another. You may be a **blood relation** of your parents, your brothers and sisters or you may be **adopted**. Your parents are not blood relations of each other. They come from two separate families. Their relationship is by marriage.

A marriage joins two families together. It starts new relationships between relatives of the husband and wife. The children of the marriage provide the next **generation** of the family. This is the part that you are playing in the story of your own family.

Among all your relations by blood or marriage, the closest to you are your parents, your brothers and sisters, and any other members of your family who share your home. You and the people you live with form a **family unit**.

Your looks come from your parents and even your grandparents. You 'take after' them, as people say. In different ways, such as your height, the colour of your hair and even the shape of your hands, you may grow to look like your parents.

▽ **Traditionally, the first step to building a family is a marriage, like this one in Japan.**

△ Do you think the children in this Brazilian family look like their parents? What do you notice about people's faces as they get older?

This happens through what scientists call **heredity**. From long before you were born, heredity was at work on how you look now and even what you will look like when you are older.

There is another **influence** at work in the family. It comes mainly from your parents, but also from any other people at home. Without thinking about it, you copy the **behaviour** of those around you. So you may not only have the same colour hair as one of your parents, you may even have the same kind of smile or frown and you may speak in the same way.

In all kinds of ways, family life helps to make us the people we are. When we eat together, watch television as a family, or go for an outing with our families we are making our family relationships stronger. That is why it is important for a family to find time to do things together.

△ Family life can be great fun – you've always got someone to play around with. We learn a lot from our families, even when just playing.

9

FAMILY PATTERNS

Families around the world live in different ways, in groups of different sizes. Examples of each type of family can be found in almost all countries. Families are free to choose the way they want to live, though their choice will be greatly influenced by what their particular society thinks is right.

The most common pattern of family life, especially in **developing countries**, is called the **extended family**. This family unit may include, as well as parents and children, grandparents and married and unmarried adult relatives. They all live together and have a place in family life. In the city, an extended family might live in a group of buildings around a central **courtyard**.

In the developed world most people live in **nuclear families**. These are made up of parents and their children who live as a separate unit with no other relations. They may see aunts, uncles, cousins and other family members frequently, but their main family relationships are with the small group of people who live in their own homes.

Thirdly, particularly in Africa and Asia, a larger kind of family is to be found. This is called the **kinship group**. It can include all the blood relations of the head of the group. A kinship group may have a whole village to itself.

▽ **This is an Indian family. When all the relations are gathered together, this seems much bigger than a nuclear family, but see page 15.**

△ **Some Sudanese families have more than one mother. This family has a grandfather, a father, two grandmothers and two mothers.**

Not all families fall neatly into one of these three types. In Britain, for example, many nuclear families live close enough to other relatives to behave in some ways like extended families, especially in looking after young children or older people. In some kinship groups, young married people spend the first years of their marriage separated from the rest of the family, so that they can get to know each other away from other people. Then, when they have children of their own, they rejoin the group.

△ **Small family units are most common in the developed world. However, families like this, with mother, father and two children are quite rare (see page 14), even in developed countries.**

11

THE EXTENDED FAMILY

Extended family life is the most common form worldwide.

In many countries there is no government help for the **unemployed**, the sick, or the elderly. They depend for support on their extended families. Those who are able to work are expected to help the others. If they go away to work they regularly send money home. In return, those members who stay at home help the family by cooking, looking after the children of working mothers, and nursing the sick.

The extended family is often essential in rural areas. At times like the harvest, a great deal of work has to be done in a short time. Living as an extended family makes it easy to call in extra help. Families that work on the land are often large, with as many as ten children. More work can be done by a larger family.

▽ **Everyone in this Indian family helps to make baskets. In this way, children can learn useful skills that they might not get a chance to learn at school. At the same time, they help the family to earn a living.**

△ In a large family there's always a spare pair of hands to help with work around the house. This Bangladeshi boy looks after his brother.

△ A family in Bangladesh at work on their farm. Large families are a help at harvest time.

If you grow up in an extended family there is never a shortage of people to discuss your worries and problems with. The different generations and relationships usually mix easily together, supporting and advising each other. But there can be cause for tension as well. In some extended families, the children and young people must always obey the older generations. And if, for any reason, the extended family is broken up, its members may find it difficult to cope without family support. This often happens in developing countries when young men have to leave the family to find work in large towns or cities (see pages 28–29).

13

THE NUCLEAR FAMILY

Most families in developed countries are nuclear, and the number of people in the world who live in nuclear families is increasing. In books and television programmes we often see families where there are a mother, a father and their children. It is easy to think that all nuclear families are like that. They are not. In the USA, less than 4 per cent of families are made up of a father who works, a mother who stays at home and two children.

There are many nuclear families with only one parent living at home. The other parent may have died, or there may have been a **divorce**. In other families there are children of two or even more marriages. Then there are nuclear families that include adopted children.

Many nuclear families keep close links with their other relations. They exchange visits at weekends, or during religious festivals like Christmas and holidays (such as Thanksgiving in the USA). They often keep in touch by letter or phone.

In the long history of the world, the nuclear family is fairly new. Up to about 200 years ago, when most people earned their living from the land, they often needed the help of all the members of their families. But in many countries today, more and more people are moving to cities, usually in search of work.

Nuclear families may be large or small. One advantage of small nuclear families is that it is easier to get around together – whether in a bus, or a car, or even a scooter! ▽

◁ **This woman looks after her son without the help of his father. Many single parents need help in looking after their children.**

People in nuclear families get a chance to meet their distant relatives at special family events – like this wedding in Portugal. ▽

When they settle in cities, large extended families tend to split up. Each family sets up on its own, in a nuclear unit. It looks as if, in the future, more children will find out what it is like to grow up in a nuclear family.

KINSHIP GROUPS

The kinship group is the largest family unit. It is made up of a number of nuclear and extended families in which many people are blood relations. The families may form the whole **population** of a village. Kinship groups are found in parts of Africa and on some of the islands of South-east Asia.

Kinship groups are the oldest kind of family organization. They exist now in places where there has been little contact with cities or industry, such as in parts of Malawi in southern Africa. One of the peoples of Malawi are the Yao. They live in kinship groups based on mother-and-daughter relationships. All the married women in a group are related to each other by blood. The men come into the group from outside, by marriage.

The Yaos are unusual. In most kinship groups it is the father-and-son relationship that is more important, and the women who are brought in by marriage. This is what happens among the Tiv people of Nigeria.

The prosperity of a kinship group depends on how many people it can feed from its land. If a Yao group produces too many daughters, it could be in trouble when they grow up and bring more men into the group. The same problem arises if a Tiv group produces too many sons – bringing in more women.

Girls and women of the Yao tribe in Malawi. Although kinship groups are less common than other family patterns, they work very successfully for the Yao. ▷

Like other kinds of families, kinship groups are put under stress when food is in short supply. In recent years, drought in Africa has brought disaster to many kinship groups.

△ A Kenyan fishing community. As in kinship groups, families work alongside one another. Here they catch fish to eat and sell.

Special camps, like these in Ethiopia, can help families, and even an entire kinship group, to stay together during a time of famine. ▷

When the crops have failed, causing a food shortage, the younger and fitter members of the groups have left in the hope of finding food somewhere else to send home. Many have died of starvation. The close-knit kinship group communities have been weakened. But for those who survive, the support of the group may prove essential in their struggle to grow and harvest the next year's crop.

HOW FAMILIES WORK

All families, if they are to live happily together, have to agree about who decides what to do. Should we move to a new house? Where shall we go on holiday? What shall we have for supper? Which TV programme shall we watch? There are all kinds of things, important and not so important, that have to be decided.

△ **Rose Kennedy is matriarch of one of the most influential political families in the USA.**

In the nuclear family, it is usually parents who decide. They may discuss things with their children and listen to their views, but in the end it is what mother and father say that counts. Of course, problems may arise when they disagree between themselves.

In the developed world, the father is often – but not always – the main **breadwinner**. Often, both parents work in order to support the family, though one will normally work part-time to be free to look after the children.

Until recently, developed countries were **patriarchal** societies. This means that people thought it was right that the father should make decisions for the family. But this is gradually changing. More women are claiming the right to have an equal say. At the same time, fewer men see themselves as the 'rulers' of their families.

△ **In many families, the grandparents have the final say on important matters. They can also help look after their grandchildren.**

Some developing countries have patriarchal societies. The male head of the family, often the grandfather, decides what is to be done. This may happen whether the men in the family are the main breadwinners or not. In many parts of Africa, women do most of the work of growing food. But it is still the men who decide what the family is to do. In some countries, in the Caribbean for example, families are usually **matriarchal**.

△ **In patriarchal societies, women are often paid less than men. These Sri Lankan tea pickers are paid little for their hard work.**

The mother or grandmother makes the decisions. Often, in these countries, the men have to go away to find work. This leaves the women in charge of the home. For most of the time, they run the family without the men's help. So when choices have to be made, it is generally the women who decide.

WHY LIVE IN A FAMILY?

Most people have an idea of what it would be like to live in a perfect family. Parents would always be kind and understanding to their children. Children would always love and respect their parents. There would be no arguments, no quarrels, no tears and no unhappiness.

In a caring family, there are hundreds of ways that we can help one another. These girls are lucky to have a sister so good at plaiting hair. ▽

Not many families are like that. But most families are like that for some of the time. And most families settle their arguments, make up their quarrels and dry their tears. People have a need to share their lives with others. We need to share pleasures with other people, and to have someone to talk to if we are frightened or worried. The family gives us a place where we can do these things.

The family can also provide work for its members. We read earlier (pages 14–15) that members of an extended family often work together on a farm or in some other business. This can happen in a nuclear family, too. For example, many nuclear families run shops, with mother, father and the children all taking part.

More often, members of a nuclear family separate their home and working lives. Putting together their earnings helps the family towards a good standard of living. One of the problems of single-parent nuclear families is that the earnings of one adult are often not enough to provide good housing, food and clothing for the single parent and the children. This is less of a problem in the extended family because other family members are there to help.

It's often at home, with the family, that children first learn to read and write. ▷

In Upper Volta, three sisters fetch water. Family life teaches us to work together. ▽

The family gives us support and love. It is a good place to run to when things in the outside world worry us. If we live in a nuclear family, one day we may want to leave and start a new nuclear family of our own. If we live in an extended family, we may have to leave it to find work. Families need to prepare their children for life outside.

FAMILY INFLUENCE

In the first years of our lives, we take our ideas of how to behave and what to think from those close to us. For most children, that means our parents. They provide us with a **model**. When we are at home, we are learning all the time without knowing it. For instance, if we live in a **violent** family, we will be more likely to accept and even use violence. If instead our parents are kind and loving to each other and to us, then we may ourselves believe that that is the way to behave.

△ **We all copy our parents without even thinking about it. When we see them happy or sad, pleased or angry, we are learning how to behave.**

The family is where children receive much of their training for life. In developing countries, where some children do not go to school, families may be the children's only source of education. Even in the developed world, children spend less than one-eighth of their time at school.

Looking after young children takes time. Who can afford to spend time on it when they need to work and earn money?

In extended families, the answer is often that grandparents bring up the children, because both parents have to go out to work. Grandparents have the time, and they have a great deal of understanding and experience to pass on. In many large extended and nuclear families the care of younger children is left to their older sisters or brothers. In families where the eldest children are mature enough, this can work reasonably well. But sometimes the older ones may be too young to take on the **responsibility**. The younger ones lose out because the older sister or brother does not have enough experience, and they may be neglected or treated badly.

There is an old saying that 'The child is father to the man'. This means that what happens to us when we are children decides what kinds of adults we will be. The best thing that can happen to us as children is that we are brought up in a secure, loving home where the people around us set a good example of how we should live.

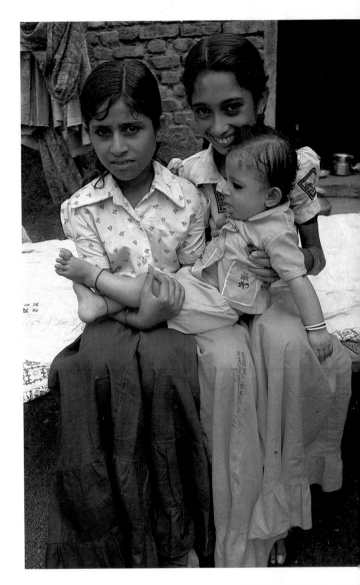

(Above right) In large families, the youngest children may be looked after by their elder brothers and sisters.

This girl plays at being a parent. She has seen her parents looking after her baby sister and wants to do the same. ▷

POVERTY

We all need to have enough to eat, a warm and comfortable home, and enough clothes to wear.

Sadly, for millions of us that is only a dream. Some people will spend all their lives in **poverty**, struggling to earn enough money for a good meal or a new coat, or to make their homes fit to live in. This struggle may prevent them and their children from enjoying a good family life.

The basic need of any family is a place in which to live. Even in developed countries like Australia many families are unable to find one. In some countries, people are forced to try to build a home out of old oil-cans and pieces of plastic sheeting. If someone wants the land to build a factory or a hotel, the poor family may have to move on. Many families spend all their lives looking for somewhere to settle down. Sometimes, they have to split up because there is nowhere for them to live together.

If you are poor, having enough to eat is the first thing you care about. A home and good health come next. Enough food is produced in the world to give everyone enough to eat. But although people in some countries eat more than they need, many children in other parts of the world go hungry and even starve to death. The **surplus** food is often in the wrong place, and the very poor are not able to buy it.

Families in poverty often suffer ill-health because of bad housing or a poor diet Quite often, their health problems can be put right with simple medicines or even with advice on how to make good, cheap meals. Save the Children has helped people to set up centres in many countries where mothers can obtain help and advice on bringing up healthy, well-fed children.

This English family is poor. They do not have adequate food, clothes or housing. ▷

A family in a slum in the Brazilian city of São Paulo. It can be very difficult to look after young children properly in such conditions. ▷

There are many poor people in India. This family in Poona has had to make a house out of materials picked up off the streets. ▽

FAMILIES IN TROUBLE

Family life should be about caring for and sharing with one another. This sometimes means thinking of someone else instead of yourself – and children as well as parents have to play their part in this. It is not always easy to live up to this example of happy family life. Parents often think that their children take up too much of their attention and leave them too little time for themselves. Children sometimes feel that they are not getting enough attention. These feelings sometimes come out in frightening and violent ways, sometimes in subtle ways – such as when small children constantly cling to their parents.

Children who feel they are not getting enough attention sometimes **rebel**. They set out to do just those things they know their parents will not like, such as behaving badly, staying out late, or even getting into trouble with the police.

△ **The Eliza Street centre in Belfast, Northern Ireland. The centre offers support for parents and play and other facilities for their children.**

△ **It is common for teenagers to argue with their parents from time to time. But if something is wrong, it's better to talk about it calmly.**

This gives them their parents' attention – but probably the wrong kind, perhaps involving cruelty. Once this happens, the family is in trouble and may need help from outside.

Families, especially nuclear families, may need outside help when parents feel they 'cannot cope'. It sometimes happens that the strain of looking after young children becomes too much. The problem is made worse if the parents are worried about money or work or poor housing. They may feel that the only answer is to go out, leaving the children alone and neglected at home.

△ **Out of school and on the streets. With no one keeping an eye on them, these two may be having fun, but they may also get into serious trouble.**

There are many agencies which try to put family life right when it has gone wrong. One example is the Eliza Street Centre in Belfast, Northern Ireland, advised by Save the Children. There, worried mothers can get help with their problems, and share with others the strain of bringing up small children with little money in cramped flats. When families find themselves in trouble, help from outside can often repair the damage.

THE LURE OF THE CITY

Every day, all over the world, young people leave their families in the country and make for the city. In the developing world, making a living from the land is hard and sometimes hopeless. Sometimes they may be moved off their land by big companies or greedy landlords. The **migrants** believe they will find well-paid work in the city. Many young people in developed countries think the same.

They are often disappointed. They find that there are no jobs to be had. There is nowhere to live. They have to put up with poor housing or even sleep rough on the street. They cannot afford – or are ashamed – to go back home.

This often brings great worry and sadness to the families of those who have left. They may wonder if they will ever hear of their loved ones again – and sometimes they never do. If a strong young person leaves a family that depends on his help on the farm, the rest will have to work harder or **employ** someone else. Then there are the questions: Why did he go? Why couldn't she have talked to us about it? Have we failed our children in some way?

In many countries migrants leave to seek work in the city with family agreement. If possible, he or she sends money back to the family.

Young people drawn by the bright lights of the city are not the only ones who leave home. Lesotho is a state in southern Africa. The farming there is very hard and there is no other work.

△ **The bright lights of Tokyo attract many poor people from small towns and rural areas. But city life can be very hard, especially if you are used to the support and friendship of a family.**

28

△ If it is not possible to find work in a city, parents may send out their children to beg. This Brazilian boy begs from cars in São Paulo.

For some poor people in cities, there is little difference between working and begging. This Indian girl will spend all day selling fruit. ▷

Many men have to go to South Africa to find jobs in the mines. They send money home, and come back on holiday once a year. If they could find work at home, most of the migrants would prefer to stay there and enjoy family life.

The world's cities are growing. There are too few homes or jobs for the people who live there. It is easy for newcomers to sink into poverty and crime. There is a great need for us to work out ways of making the countryside a better place to live in to encourage people to stay there.

FAMILIES UPROOTED

For thirty years, until 1975, there was war in Vietnam. In 1975, South Vietnam was defeated. Over the next few years, hundreds of thousands of South Vietnamese families fled their country, fearing what would happen to them if they stayed. Some walked across the border into neighbouring countries. More left by boat, hoping to land on a friendly shore. Many of them drowned.

Floods are common in Bangladesh. Overnight the family home may be wrecked. Sometimes it may be necessary to move to a new place. ▽

Vietnamese **refugees** were just one of the many groups of families who have been uprooted from their homes by war, famine, or governments that simply want to get rid of them. They have left their homes, and their only hope is that some friendly country will take them in and give them the chance to build a new life. Since 1978, more than 280,000 Vietnamese refugees have been settled in China, and others have settled in countries further away like Japan and the USA.

However, where possible, the best situation is where people are helped to return to their homeland.

Refugees usually move in a panic. Parents lose sight of their children, and children of their parents. When they arrive in a new country, they cannot speak the language. They are frightened. They have no money and often no clothes except for what they are wearing. They are worried about members of their families that they have left behind.

Some refugee families are able to settle down in their new countries. They find homes and work, and slowly get over the shock of what has happened to them. But others do not. They will be worried for the rest of their lives by questions that they cannot answer. Did my mother and father manage to get away? What happened to my eldest son? Is there any chance that I will ever see them again?

Meanwhile, refugee families need help to live with their past and settle into new lives. Many do so with great success, often helped by the United Nations High Commissioner for Refugees which works around the world to help people to rebuild their lives, safe from danger and persecution. The refugee families who have been through this and survived show how strong the family can be.

△ **Vietnamese refugees in Hong Kong. Despite the problems facing them, many Vietnamese families have settled successfully.**

Refugees from Honduras are sheltered in a camp in Mexico. Such camps are essential for people who have fled from their homes. ▽

DISABILITY IN THE FAMILY

Everyone in a family has something to give to family life. All of us can do some things particularly well, but can do other things less well. We are all different in this way.

Some people cannot do certain things. Perhaps they do not see, hear, walk or speak, or are unable to learn quickly; these people are called disabled. People who don't walk become disabled by things like steps, which wheelchairs can't go up, or narrow doors which they can't pass through, so they need ramps and wider doors. People who don't hear become disabled when they try and listen to the radio or TV, but hearing aids, subtitles and microphones will help. People who don't speak clearly become disabled when others don't listen properly to what they have to say; so, we need to listen carefully.

People with disabilities can have fun just like anyone else. With help from his friends, this boy takes part in a ball game. ▽

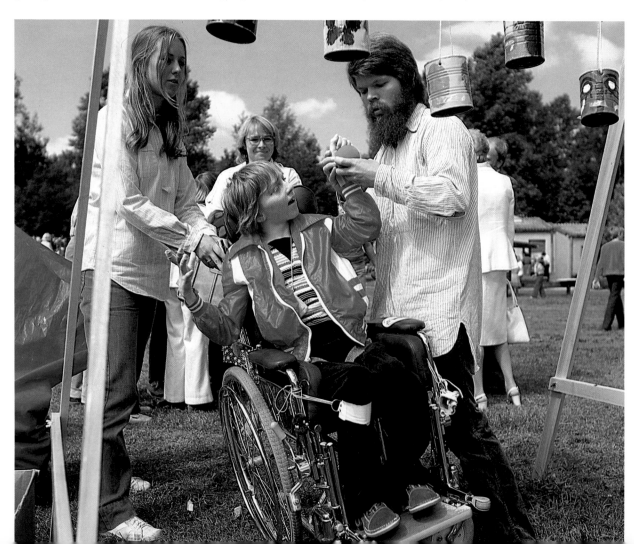

△ Many people with disabilities take up a variety of sports activities, like horse riding.

△ This man can work as well as anyone at this computer terminal, which means that as far as his work is concerned he is not 'disabled' at all.

Disabled people want to be accepted just as they are at home, in school, or wherever else they may be. They are no different from anybody else in wanting to take part in as many activities as they can. There are many ways in which this can be made possible. For example, if someone in your family uses a wheelchair, make sure you ask them first what sort of help they need. If someone in your family has a hearing aid, make sure you speak slowly and that they can see your lips when you speak to them. Listen carefully to their reply – some deaf people may not be able to speak very clearly.

One person out of every ten is disabled. Disabled children have the same hopes as everyone else of living full lives, with satisfying jobs and families of their own. Unfortunately, life is more difficult for them. Activities that most people find easy like travelling to work, or going shopping, become a problem for disabled people. We can all help change this. Perhaps a friend in your class has a brother or sister who is deaf. You could help by learning some sign language – ask your teacher to help. If you do this and other things, then the people you meet and people in your family will become less disabled.

33

THE DAMAGED FAMILY

Everyone who marries hopes for happiness, and most people who marry expect to create a happy family. Sadly, not every marriage is successful, and not every family is happy. Some marriages end in **separation** or divorce, when the husband and wife part and lead separate lives. If there are children, they usually (but not always) stay with their mother. Other marriages end with the death of one of the partners.

△ **If your parents separate or get divorced, you may have to get used to having one parent look after you instead of two.**

In Canada about one in eight of all families are single-parent families. In most of these, the parent is the mother. Not all are families where there has been a separation or a divorce. Some single-parent mothers are **widows**, and some have chosen not to marry the father of their children.

The loss of a parent, whether by divorce or death, is a shock to the rest of the family. Money worries may add to the sadness. It is often hard for children to understand what has happened. At times like this, children need the support of the remaining parent – and of their friends and other members of the wider family. Young children and their mothers or fathers often turn for help to agencies like Save the Children which run playgroups and family centres.

Most families damaged by divorce or death do get over the shock and manage to put their lives back together. Divorced or widowed parents often marry again, joining their own family with another.

In countries where the extended family is the normal pattern, divorce takes place less often. It is easier in an extended family for their children to be looked after because other relatives are on hand to help.

Sometimes divorce cannot be avoided. But in fact most families stay together. Most people work hard to keep their marriages and their families happy, because they believe that is the best way to live.

Save the Children runs this family project in Clacton, England. The project offers a safe place for children to play and an opportunity for their parents to meet and seek advice. ▽

'NEW' FAMILIES

If divorced or widowed parents marry again, they may bring together the children of their earlier marriages. When this happens, a new set of relationships is created. This is how it can work.

Jane is divorced from the father of Tom and Sue. John is divorced from the mother of Sally and Peter. Jane marries John, and so there will be four children in their family. Tom and Sue become the stepbrother and stepsister of Sally and Peter. John becomes Tom's and Sue's stepfather, and Jane becomes Sally's and Peter's stepmother. All these relationships are called **step-relationships**.

◁ **These orphans from Ethiopia lost their families during a famine. If they are adopted they may receive the care and love that they need.**

A death in the family is always hard to bear. But it can change those who remain, as they form new, closer relationships with one another. ▽

John and Jane should take care that none of the children feels less loved than the others. They must make sure that everyone has a say when they are deciding what to do as a family. Unless all four children receive a fair share of attention, some of them will feel jealous of the others.

Another kind of 'new' family is made if a husband and wife decide to adopt one or more children. This may happen if the husband and wife are not able to have children of their own, or want more but cannot have them. Adoption is a way of giving a loving home to a child who cannot be looked after by his or her own parents. The new parents, who are called the adoptive parents, bring the child up as their own, and give him or her their family name.

It sometimes happens that, perhaps because of illness, parents cannot look

△ **A loving family with parents and brothers and sisters may be an impossible dream for some orphans; but for those who are adopted it is as possible as it is for any other children.**

after their children for a time, and the children go to live with **foster-parents**. Foster-parents take children into their homes and look after them, but they know that once the problem is sorted out the children will go back to their own families. In this way they are different to adoptive parents.

Children who are adopted or fostered need to be treated with as much love and care as they would be by their own parents. Sadly, this is not always the case. Not every fostering is successful, and some children are passed unhappily from one family to another. All families, including 'new' families, only work well when they are made up of people who are committed to caring for one another.

37

CHAPTER 4: ALTERNATIVES TO THE FAMILY
COMMUNAL LIVING

Although most people live in a family, it is not the only way of living in a group.

Many people in Israel live in kibbutzim. These are farming villages where being part of the community is more important than being part of a family. In most kibbutzim, families do not live together. Children are brought up in separate 'houses' with other children of their own age. They see their parents for about two hours each day, and at weekends. When they are eighteen, they join the other adults and have their own rooms. When they come in from work all the adults have their meals together in the kibbutz dining-room.

Another kind of group living is the commune. This is usually made up of a number of nuclear families, not related to one another, who share a large house or a number of houses. They have their own rooms to sleep in, but come together for meals, games and television. The men and women of the commune share the cooking, cleaning and washing, and the care of the children. Some communes live on what they can produce in their gardens, but in others some of the members go out to work.

Children in a kibbutz in Israel are looked after during the day by an adult member of the community – out of harm's way! ▽

People who enjoy living in communes say that it is more fun to be part of a large group than to be shut up as a nuclear family in a small house. In some communes the children are taught at home instead of going to school.

However, communes do not suit everyone; some people dislike the idea of sharing their lives and property with people outside their families. For children, living in a commune is similar to growing up in an extended family or in a large nuclear family. There is always someone to play with or talk to – but it might be difficult if you wanted to be on your own for a while.

These children in Norfolk, England, live in a commune. In the background you can see the large house that is shared by several families. ▽

Some of the world's poorest people are forced into a kind of communal living, as here in a shanty town in Manila, in the Philippines. ▽ (Bottom)

ON YOUR OWN

In the USA, about one out of every ten people lives on his or her own. Some have been widowed or divorced. Some have never met anyone they want to live with. Others live on their own because that is what they have chosen to do.

In most developing countries, this would be thought very strange. There, single people live with other members of their families. Widows and **widowers** go to live with one of their adult children. If you are used to being part of a busy, lively family it is very hard to live alone. This is one of the problems faced by young people in developing countries who move to the cities.

Not many years ago, people in countries like Britain or Australia thought it strange for anyone except for widows and widowers to live alone. Young people were expected to get married and start families. If they did not, it was a sign of failure. Everyone felt sorry for them. The result was that many young people married too soon, or married although they did not really want to.

This woman lives on her own. She has learned to look after herself without having family or a friend around to help her. People like her are not necessarily lonely. They may prefer independence to family life. ▽

Today, things are changing. Young people do not feel that they must get married. The age when people marry is slowly rising. No one thinks it strange if several people share a home, but live their own separate lives. There are many different ways of living, and family life is only one of them.

There are many reasons for these changes. One is that more young people become students, and find that they enjoy the freedom of student lifestyle. Another is that it is difficult for a young married couple to find a home that they can afford. **Unemployment** is another reason. Few people are prepared to risk starting a family if there is no work to support it.

There is no rule that people must live in families. What is important is that if they choose to do so, they try hard to create a happy family for all its members.

△ **This teenager left his family to look for work in London, England. He now lives alone in a damp room in the bed-and-breakfast hotel behind him.**

In big, busy cities, like Hong Kong, it can be difficult for newcomers to make new friends, and they may end up living alone for some time. ▽

FUTURE FAMILIES

The family has changed a great deal throughout history. It is still changing.

In richer countries, families are very much smaller than they were 100 years ago. Their homes are less crowded and more comfortable. People are healthier and better fed.

In developed countries, family life has changed. Parents share the jobs around the house more equally than they have before. They take more notice of what their children think. Fathers spend more time with their children.

Families in the developing world are also changing. As many families move to the cities, some remain together as extended families while many others split apart to become nuclear families.

What will families be like in another 100 years? Of course, we can only guess. But if we look at the changes that have already taken place, it can be a fairly good guess. At the moment, more and more people are moving to cities. If this continues to happen, families will gradually become smaller. With improvements in medicine, more parents will choose to have just one or two children, knowing that they will have a good chance of survival. With the help of **contraception**, parents are able to plan their families. In order to help control population increase, the governments of some countries (like that in China) encourage parents to have small families.

Small families, like this one in Peking, China, may become increasingly common around the world. ▽

△ Whatever else changes in the world, children, like these in Sri Lanka, will continue to need their families.

Perhaps the best way to plan for the future is to look after the children of today. This couple will one day need looking after themselves! ▷

It may be that the smaller nuclear families, with one child each, will choose to live together in pairs or larger groups, rather like small communes. This would help to make full use of houses built for larger families.

One thing we can be sure of – the family will carry on. It has lasted for thousands of years, and for most of us there is no better way of living.

GLOSSARY

Adopted Taken into a family, but not blood-related.

Behaviour How people behave.

Blood relation A person related to another by birth, not by marriage.

Breadwinner Someone who earns money by working.

Contraception A method used to prevent a woman becoming pregnant during sexual intercourse.

Courtyard An open space surrounded by buildings.

Developing countries Poorer countries that do not yet have the housing, work opportunities, education or health care that rich countries, or developed countries, take for granted.

Divorce The ending of a marriage by law.

Employ Give work to.

Experience Knowledge of life.

Extended family A family which includes relations of the parents and children, often spanning more than three generations.

Family unit Any family living together.

Foster-parents A couple who look after a child that is not their own.

Generation A group of people of about the same age.

Heredity The passing-on of looks and character from parents to children.

Influence The effects of one person or thing on another

Kinship group A group of people related by blood to the head of the group.

Matriarchal A group or society taking leadership from the mother.

Migrants People who leave one place to live in another.

Model Example.

Nuclear family A family made up of parents, children, and sometimes grandparents.

Patriarchal A group or society taking leadership from the father.

Population All the people who live in a country or place.

Poverty Not having enough food, or adequate housing or money to pay for life's essentials.

Rebel To refuse to obey people who think they can tell you what to do.

Refugees People who have to move to a new area or country because of famine or war.

Relationships Links between people.

Responsibility Duty.

Separation When a husband and wife decide to live apart.

Step-relationship A relationship between members of the family brought about by more than one marriage.

Surplus More than is required.

Survival Staying alive.

Unemployment Being unable to find work.

Violent Using force.

Widow A woman whose husband has died.

Widower A man whose wife has died

TEACHERS' NOTES

The family as a classroom topic must be treated sensitively, as many of the situations mentioned in this book, such as divorce, bereavement, adoption and fostering, will have been experienced by some of the pupils in most classes. (This is of course not to say that they should not be discussed, as long as the teacher is aware of possible problems.) At the same time, the family is an experience common to all, and so every child can make a contribution.

The aim of this book is to take a positive view of family life, despite the problems that cannot be avoided. Many broken homes are mended. Most parents do love and care for their children. Most families are, on the whole, happy. It seems important to stress this at a time when there is so much media emphasis on the family's faults and failings.

The conventional distinction between the 'nuclear' and the 'extended' family can be misleading. It is important that the children of nuclear families don't think that the extended family is some strange set-up that happens in other countries. Some elements of extended family life, such as baby-sitting by grandmother or staying with an aunt while a new baby is awaited, will be familiar to many children. Such incidents can be highlighted to emphasize that many aspects of family life are part of the worldwide experience of children.

It is difficult for some children to grasp concepts of relationship, especially if they are confused by the habit of calling mere friends of the family 'auntie' and 'uncle', and by the many variants used to address grandparents. The step-relationships described on pages 36–37 may cause particular difficulty. It is worth remembering that every class contains a full cast of actors for use in demonstrations!

Possibilities for drama and story-writing linked to this book include:

● The situation of a young man or woman in an African village who decides to go to the city.
● Harvest-time on a farm owned by an extended family.
● The problems of a Bangladeshi couple living in Britain.
● A (nuclear) family discussing whether to move, and what kind of house to look for.
● A family quarrel about what time children should be home.

It is possible to touch on such issues as the single-parent family without involving divorce, separation or widowhood by discussing the situation in many families where one parent is away during the week, or for longer periods, at work. This is a common situation in the happiest of families (parents in the armed services, building contractors, salespeople, long-distance lorry drivers, for example.

Bearing in mind that the family is the nearest most of us can approach the concept of history, a project based on family memories can be rewarding. At its most ambitious, this could include family snapshots from different generations, recordings of older members of the family, and an exhibition of artefacts. More simply, it could be merely a collection of anecdotes ('My mum remembers when . . .'; 'My grandad was in the War.').

Finally, a plea on behalf of the organizations listed on page 46. They welcome enquiries from schools but urge teachers to nominate *one* child as the class correspondent, and to ensure that adequate return stamps are enclosed. Letters addressed to the Schools Department will usually reach the right person fastest.

USEFUL ADDRESSES

Local sources of literature and information including Citizens' Advice Bureaux (listed in the phone book), the information or social services departments of local authorities, and of course public libraries, which often display leaflets on family affairs.

Many organizations produce information packs or other teaching materials:

Catholic Fund for Overseas Development (CAFOD), 2 Garden Close, Stockwell Road, London SW9 9TY.

Centre for World Development Education, Regent's College, Regent's Park, London NW1 4NS.

Christian Aid, PO Box 1, London SW9 8BH.

Christian Education Movement, Lancaster House, Borough Road, Isleworth, Middlesex TW7 5DU.

Commonwealth Institute, Kensington High Street, London W8 8NQ.

Council for Education in World Citizenship, Seymour Mews House, Seymour Mews, London W1H 9PE.

Hampshire Development Education Centre, Mid-Hants Teachers' Centre, Elm Road, Winchester, Hampshire SO22 5AG.

National Society for the Prevention of Cruelty to Children, 1 Riding House Street, London W1P 8AA. (Child Protection Line: (01) 404–4447)

National Children's Bureau, 8 Wakeley Street, London EC1V 7QE.

Overseas Development Administration, Information Department, Room E920, Eland House, Stag Place, London SW1.

OXFAM, Oxfam House, 274 Banbury Road, Oxford OX2 7DZ.

Population Concern, 231 Tottenham Court Road, London W1.

Save the Children, Mary Datchelor House, 17 Grove Lane, London SE5 8RD.

Shelter (The National Campaign for the Homeless), 157 Waterloo Road, London SE1.

UNICEF, 55–56 Lincoln's Inn Fields, London WC2A 3NB.

War on Want, 37–39 Great Guildford Street, London SE1 0ES.

World Development Movement, Bedford Chambers, Covent Garden, London WC2E 8HA.

Other organizations concerned with family affairs include:

Cruse (The national organization for the widowed and their children), 126 Sheen Road, Richmond, Surrey.

Families Anonymous, 88 Caledonian Road, London N1.

Family Service Units, 207 Old Marylebone Road, London NW1.

Families need Fathers, Elfrida Hall, Camphill Road, London SE13.

Help the Aged, St James's Walk, London EC1.

MIND (National Association for Mental Health), 22 Harley Street, London W1.

Mothers' Union, Mary Sumner House, Tufton Street, London SW1.

National Council for One-Parent Families, 255 Kentish Town Road, London NW5.

National Federation of Women's Institutes, 39 Eccleston Square, London SW1.

National Stepfamily Association, Maris House, Maris Lane, Trumpington Road, Cambridge.

BOOKS TO READ

CHILDREN'S NON-FICTION ON FAMILY THEMES

A closer look at . . . series (Hamish Hamilton)
Subjects include the Inuit, Amazonian
Indians and other original peoples, with
useful information on family and social
structures.

Families around the world series (Wayland).
19 studies of family life in developed and
developing countries ranging from Australia
to Thailand.

Family Life by Olivia Bennett (Macmillan
Education, 1982). Accounts of family life in a
variety of settings, urban and rural, in
developed and developing countries. In the
same series and also useful: *City Life* and
Village Life.

Family Life by J. Mayled (Wayland, 1986).
Sets the events of family life in a variety of
religious contexts.

Patterns of Living by Michael Pollard (Holt,
Rinehart and Winston, 1985). Deals with
changes in, and influences on, family life in
Britain during this century.

CHILDREN'S FICTION ON FAMILY THEMES

For younger readers
(Puffin paperbacks)

A dog so small by Philippa Pearce.

Carrie's war by Nina Bawden.

The house of sixty fathers by Meindert
deJong.

The silver sword by Ian Serrailleur.

For older readers
(Puffin paperbacks)

It's like this, cat by Emily Neville.

Little house in the big woods and other titles.
by Laura Ingalls Wilder.

Lottie and Lisa by Erich Kastner.

Magnolia Buildings by Elizabeth Stucley.

Torrie by Annabel and Edgar Johnson.

FOR TEACHERS
Oxfam and the Centre for World
Development Education (see page 46 for
addresses) have extensive catalogues of
material, including teachers' guides.

World Studies 8–13 by Simon Fisher and
David Hicks (Oliver and Boyd, 1986).

PICTURE CREDITS

INDEX

Page numbers that refer to pictures are in **bold**.